How to Write

Writing a Report

by Nick Rebman

www.focusreaders.com

Focus Readers is distributed by North Star Editions:
sales@northstareditions.com | 888-417-0195

Produced for Focus Readers by Red Line Editorial.

Photographs ©: Shutterstock Images, cover, 1, 4, 7, 8, 10, 13, 14–15, 16, 21, 22, 24, 29; iStockphoto, 19; Red Line Editorial, 27 (report); Tom Fisk/Pexels, 27 (eagle)

Library of Congress Cataloging-in-Publication Data
Names: Rebman, Nick, author.
Title: Writing a report / by Nick Rebman.
Description: Mendota Heights, MN : Focus Readers, 2024. | Series: How to write | Includes index. | Audience: Grades 2-3
Identifiers: LCCN 2023029421 (print) | LCCN 2023029422 (ebook) | ISBN 9798889980247 (hardcover) | ISBN 9798889980674 (paperback) | ISBN 9798889981503 (pdf) | ISBN 9798889981107 (ebook)
Subjects: LCSH: Report writing--Juvenile literature.
Classification: LCC LB1047.3 .R435 2024 (print) | LCC LB1047.3 (ebook) | DDC 371.30281--dc23/eng/20230725
LC record available at https://lccn.loc.gov/2023029421
LC ebook record available at https://lccn.loc.gov/2023029422

Printed in the United States of America
Mankato, MN
012024

About the Author

Nick Rebman is a writer and editor who lives in Minnesota.

Table of Contents

Chapter 1

Ready to Write

A girl has to write a report for school. She is interested in **renewable energy**. But she knows this topic is large. There are many kinds of renewable energy. So, she decides to be more specific.

Many people use the internet when they're exploring ideas to write about.

Her report will focus only on solar farms.

The girl starts by doing **research**. She finds articles online. She takes notes as she reads them. Then, she puts the notes in an order that makes sense.

Did You Know?

Many people prefer to write on a computer. That way, they can fix mistakes easily. They can also move ideas around.

 Solar farms are better for the environment than coal-powered plants. They also cost less.

First, she will **define** what solar farms are. Next, she will explain how they make electricity. Then, she will list why they are helpful. The girl is excited to share what she has learned.

Chapter 2

Doing Research

First, choose a topic to focus on for your report. Make sure the topic isn't too big. For example, suppose you love birds. There are many types of birds. Writing about them all would be nearly impossible.

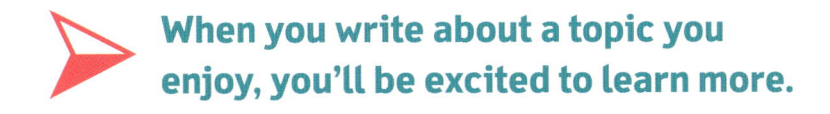 **When you write about a topic you enjoy, you'll be excited to learn more.**

 Librarians can help you find the information you are looking for.

Instead, you could choose one bird.

You could write your report about

bald eagles.

You'll need lots of information about your topic. So, the next step is to do research. The library is a great place to start. A web search can also provide good information.

Take notes as you read your **sources**. You can use notecards, paper, or a computer. Your notes shouldn't include every detail you read. Only write facts and ideas related to your report's topic.

Also, your notes should say where you found the information.

One source might be a book. In this case, write down the title, author, and page number. Another source might be from the internet. In this case, write down the website and the title of the article.

Suppose you find a book about how birds hunt. If your report is

 When you take notes, don't copy sentences from your source. Instead, use your own words.

about bald eagles, don't write down facts about falcons or hawks. Just take notes on bald eagles. One note might say, "Bald eagles often hunt for fish. <u>Birds of Prey</u> by Jane Smith. Page 27."

Reliable Sources

Make sure your sources are **reliable**. This is especially important if you're using websites. Sites ending with .edu or .gov are usually reliable. However, social media isn't. Blogs aren't either. If you're unsure about a source, ask a teacher or librarian.

Also, don't rely too much on a single source. It might be **biased** or incomplete. Instead, use several sources. That way, you'll get different points of view.

Finally, use information that is up to date. Try to avoid sources that are several years old.

Website endings are called domain extensions.

Chapter 3

Organizing and Writing

After you finish your research, read through all your notes. Look for similar types of information. Put these notes together in groups. For instance, some notes might be about bald eagles' bodies.

 Similar to physical items, ideas can be grouped by what they have in common.

Put those notes in one group. Put the notes about diet in another. And put the notes about their life cycle in another group. Each group can be one of your report's main ideas.

Now it's time to write the **first draft**. Always begin with an

Did You Know?

Remember to use your notes. You can also look back at your sources. That way, you'll find any extra details that you need.

 Try to include three to five main ideas in your report.

introduction. This **paragraph** tells readers what the report is about. The first few sentences should make readers interested. The next sentences will state your main ideas.

Next, write a separate paragraph for each main idea. The first sentence should describe the idea. For instance, it might say, "Bald eagles have many body parts that help them hunt."

The rest of the paragraph should give supporting details. The details may show why the first sentence is true. Or they may add extra information. For example, a supporting detail may say, "Sharp claws help eagles grab food."

The last paragraph should be a conclusion. This section should **summarize** the main ideas. It should also remind readers why your topic is important.

Chapter 4

Editing

After you write your first draft, set it aside. Come back a day or two later. Read through the whole report. You will probably notice some mistakes. That's normal. Now it's time to edit.

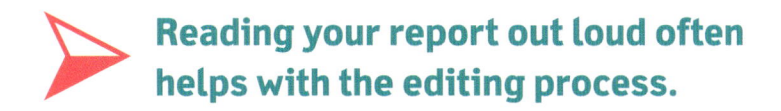 **Reading your report out loud often helps with the editing process.**

 **If the information doesn't flow well, try putting some sentences in a different order.**

Start by focusing on bigger ideas. For instance, think about how your report is organized. All the information should flow smoothly. After that, you can pay attention to smaller details. Make sure your report uses linking words. These words connect your ideas. They show that two sentences are related. Examples include *also*, *plus*, and *however*.

Also, define key words. Suppose you mention talons. You could explain that talons are sharp claws.

Did You Know?

Pictures and graphs can be helpful in reports. Images can make some information easier to understand.

Next, list all your sources. That way, your reader will know where you found your information. For each source, include the author and title. If the source was a book, include the page number as well. The list of sources should go at the end of your report.

Finally, check your spelling. Then read your report one last time. When everything is finished, print a copy. Now it's time to share your report with others!

PARTS OF A REPORT

linking word

helpful image

Bald Eagles

introduction

Bald eagles are important in the United States. They are the country's national bird. However, many Americans don't know much about bald eagles. There is a lot to learn about their bodies, diet, and life cycle.

main idea

definition

supporting detail

Bald eagles have many body parts that help them hunt. For example, bald eagles have talons. Talons are sharp claws. Sharp claws help eagles grab food.

Bald eagles hunt a variety of animals. They often hunt for fish. But bald eagles eat dead animals, too. They also hunt other birds and small animals.

A bald eagle's life cycle starts as an egg. The egg hatches after about a month. Baby bald eagles start out with their mother. They learn to fly. Learning takes a few months. Then, another month passes. After that, bald eagles can live on their own.

conclusion

In conclusion, bald eagles are fascinating birds. That's because their bodies are built to hunt. Also, they eat many kinds of animals. Finally, they go from egg to adult in several months. Hopefully, more Americans will learn about bald eagles.

Sources:

list of sources

1. Birds of Prey by Jane Smith. Pages 27–29.

2. "Bald Eagle Fact Sheet." US Fish & Wildlife Service. https://www.fws.gov/sites/default/files/documents/bald-eagle-fact-sheet.pdf.

FOCUS ON
Writing a Report

Write your answers on a separate piece of paper.

1. Summarize the main ideas of Chapter 2.

2. Which topic are you most interested in writing about? Why?

3. What should the conclusion do?
   - **A.** include biased information
   - **B.** summarize the main ideas
   - **C.** list all the sources

4. Why should you avoid a source that is 25 years old?
   - **A.** The source probably doesn't have page numbers.
   - **B.** The source probably wasn't written by an expert.
   - **C.** The source probably has information that is out of date.

5. What does **specific** mean in this book?

*So, she decides to be more **specific**. Her report will focus only on solar farms.*

    A. focused on many things

    B. focused on one thing

    C. focused on nothing

6. What does **rely** mean in this book?

*Also, don't **rely** too much on a single source. It might be biased or incomplete. Instead, use several sources.*

    A. to depend on

    B. to disagree with

    C. to get rid of

Answer key on page 32.

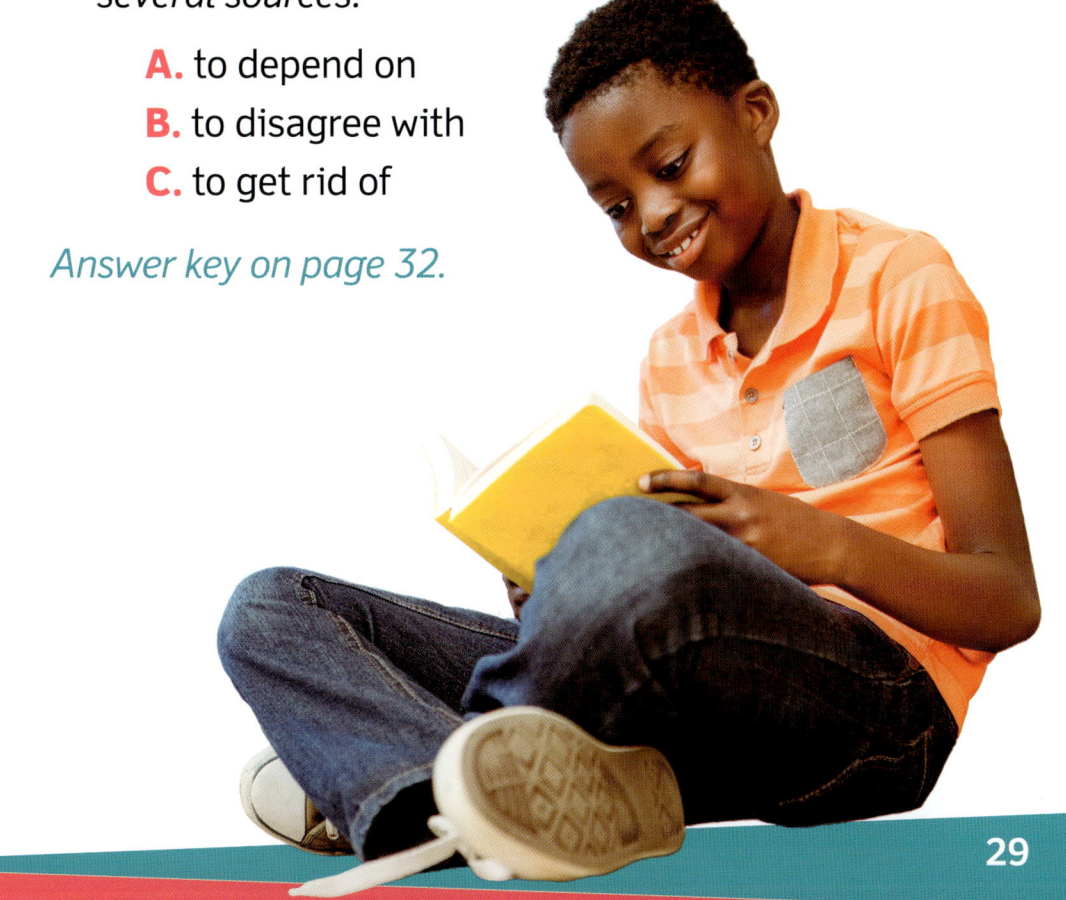

Glossary

biased
Supporting one idea over another, often unfairly.

define
To explain what a word means.

first draft
The earliest form of a piece of writing. It will be changed and improved later.

paragraph
A part of a longer piece of writing that covers one idea and usually has more than one sentence.

reliable
Able to be trusted.

renewable energy
Energy produced from a source that will not run out.

research
The act of studying something to learn more about it.

sources
Places where information comes from, such as books, websites, and newspapers.

summarize
To explain the main idea of a longer piece of writing.

To Learn More

BOOKS

Eason, Sarah, and Louise Spilsbury. *How Do I Write Well?* Shrewsbury, UK: Cheriton Children's Books, 2022.

Heinrichs, Ann. *Similes and Metaphors*. Mankato, MN: The Child's World, 2020.

Minden, Cecilia, and Kate Roth. *Writing a Report*. Ann Arbor, MI: Cherry Lake Publishing, 2019.

NOTE TO EDUCATORS

Visit **www.focusreaders.com** to find lesson plans, activities, links, and other resources related to this title.

Index

A
articles, 6, 12
author, 12, 26

C
conclusion, 21, 27

E
editing, 23–26

F
first draft, 18, 23

I
information, 11, 14, 17, 20, 24–26
introduction, 18–19, 27

K
key words, 25

L
linking words, 25, 27

M
main ideas, 18–21, 27

N
notes, 6, 11, 13, 17–18

P
paragraph, 19–21

R
research, 6, 11–13, 14, 17

S
sources, 11–13, 14, 18, 26–27
spelling, 26
supporting details, 20, 27

T
topic, 5, 9, 11, 21

Answer Key: 1. Answers will vary; **2.** Answers will vary; **3.** B; **4.** C; **5.** B; **6.** A